Climb Out of Life's Back Seat
and Step into your God-given Purpose

Table of Contents

Dedicated to my children: Juliet, Honor, and Jason. I pray that you each find your purpose and path beyond the many hurdles and obstacles of this life.

Thank you to Dennia. We make a dope team.

"You don't have a life, you are life." Eckhart Tolle

Introduction

One of my favorite movies is the 1985 classic "Back To The Future." Yep, I said 1985, so forgive me upfront for the old school reference, but if you haven't seen the movie, you should go watch it as soon as you finish this book. In the flick, the two main characters, Marty McFly and Doc Brown, experiment with time travel. They are able to use plutonium as fuel to launch Marty and the space vehicle they built back into the past. Stuck in the past with no plutonium, Marty and a young Doc Brown rely on their knowledge that the town they live in is well-known for its clock tower, which was destroyed by a bolt of lightning in the past. In the climax of the movie, they perfectly time the strike and drive the vehicle up to the doomed tower. They tie a hook to the clock's hands when the big storm hits, electricity from the lightning is sent down from the clock tower by a wire and into Doc Brown's device called a 'flux capacitor' that is fueling the uniquely designed vehicle (a 1982 DeLorean DMC-12) Marty is relying on to shoot him back into the present time—not really OUR present time, but back to the 1985 present (yeah, old school, I know).

Since you are reading this literary masterpiece, that means you are alive and (just like Marty McFly and that dope, silver DeLorean) you are traveling through time in a uniquely designed vehicle. You are also fueled by a blinding and mysterious power that's passing through you. Except instead of bouncing around back and forth through time, you are travelling only forward, one day at a time. Your *vehicle* is your life. The power fueling is the mind-blowing power of God.

Right now, your heart is beating about eighty times every minute. At the same time, your brain is translating the words on this page into thoughts and ideas in your mind. That means you are alive and you have purpose. We all do. Part of *my* purpose is to write this book and leave you with a message that God made clear to me. I can't know the exact impact this book will have on you in particular, but I do know that writing it is part of *my* journey—part of the work I have to do on my own straight line through time in my own vehicle of a body. My journey was destined to meet you in your journey right here at this point. The words on this page may be the only point that I will ever cross paths with you. We are passing by each other in the parade of life and neither one of us can be the same after this day.

In my 2014 book, *The Poet Who Watched The Whole Parade*, I detailed the pain of experiencing the death of my mother, father, brother, uncle, and grandmother. What I learned in walking back through that pain is that I wasn't a victim; I was just the person who was born to experience them. I was the one God designed to live on to tell their stories and help people find Him through those stories. My loved ones had done their job in life, now it was my turn. I had to begin the hard work of finding my purpose and making my experiences become a living testimony. I had to begin allowing life to fully happen *through* me, and quit believing the sob story that life and its cruel ways had happened *to* me. I had to allow myself to be used for God's work. So if my life was truly the vehicle, I decided to harness God's power to get back to my own future. I decided to get in the driver's seat.

The purpose of this book is to help you make that same jump into the driver's seat of your life and start driving towards not just your personal goals, but your God-ordained purpose. I know we have all heard the terms "being driven" and "having drive" thrown around as positive descriptions of successful people. Well, in order to *be* driven or to *have* drive, we have to figure out how to do our part in that. We have to be in that Driver's Seat.

This book is designed to help you get into the Driver's Seat of your own life *right now*—no more excuses, hesitation and no more allowing fear to cripple you. If you want to live your life to the fullest, let's hit the gas!

Chapter 1

The Vehicle

"For we are his workmanship, created in Christ Jesus unto good works, which God hath before ordained that we should walk in them." (Ephesians 2:10)

The Present of "the present"

I know for a fact that every one of you reading this has been watching TV at some point during the holiday season and seen one of those "car as a gift" commercials that get played every year, right around the holiday season. You know the type of ad I'm talking about; it almost always starts off with the camera winding around the curvy driveway outside the flossy suburban home of some obviously wealthy family. As the scene plays out, we usually see a son or daughter or wife (never husband) being led out of the door to be surprised by a brand new car sitting in the driveway wrapped in a ridiculously large red bow (always red). The new-car-getter, we'll call them that, starts to smile ear to ear and gush over the vehicle they just received as a present. The camera pans in a circle to show the car at every angle, not one spot or blemish on it, just gleaming in the sun. Just from watching the commercial, we get jealous of that family and start wishing we lived like that and wishing we were the ones coming out of that house and getting that expensive gift. I know I have felt like that my entire life when seeing that kinda stuff thrown in my face.

But when it really boils down to the things that truly matter in life, we DO live that reality and we DO have that type of gift. As a matter of fact, we all woke up this morning to it. Follow me, now because I know most y'all didn't roll out of a huge bed in a lavish home, *but* we all were granted this day of our own unique blessed life. We probably didn't walk outside into a turnaround driveway and find a new car with a bow on it, *but* we did wake up blessed with unique spiritual gifts and a new day gift wrapped just for us. We woke up to twenty-four hours of freshly baked opportunity to put our gifts to good use. If we start to look at every single day, every single season, every challenge or opportunity as that new gift-wrapped whip (that's a car, keep up now) gleaming in the driveway waiting for us, imagine how much different would we approach life. Imagine how much that one simple paradigm shift can begin to change our daily approach.

Workmanship

So let's make that change right now. Start waking up and looking at life like a new Benz chilling out in your driveway,

10

and feeling brand new again every morning. Now, you know that out in the real world, that shiny Benz with the pretty red bow on it will start losing value the moment you drive that bad boy just fifty feet down the driveway. Thankfully though, God's gift of a fresh day doesn't fade like that. Your value is inherent, that means it's passed directly from the One who created you and only will gain value the more you choose to align with His plan. So every day that you wake up, you instantly start writing a new page in the book of your life. You didn't choose to, God chose you. The only question is, What will today's page say for you? Will it be a blank page because you sat stagnant and didn't even try to use what you have or will it be a page that helps to build your life story into a victorious screenplay?

The given Bible quote from Ephesians 2:10 states that "...we are his workmanship, created in Christ Jesus unto good works, which God hath before ordained that we should walk in them." But what does *workmanship* really mean? The Greek word for workmanship is *poiēma*, which means "that which has been made" or "a work." It's where we get the modern word *poem*.

The ascribed writer of Ephesians, Paul of Tarsus, uses the word *poiēma* again in Romans 1:20, when he says,

> "For ever since the world was created, people have seen the earth and sky. Through *everything God made*

(poiēma), they can clearly see his invisible qualities—his eternal power and divine nature. So they have no excuse for not knowing God."

Here, Paul says that we can see God's invisible qualities manifest through "everything God made" or workmanship...*poiēma*. So if we are part of the "everything God made" then, each one of our lives is something God has made for a purpose—to manifest his own power and nature. Paul makes it even more impactful when he ends by saying that because of His *poiēma*, no one has an excuse for not knowing God. We are a part of the way God expresses Himself. We are *not* meaningless. Your life is *not* insignificant. It's the opposite! You just being alive is a vehicle that God is using specifically for His purposes. There is a specific work to do that only you can do! Right now, remind yourself that you are a DeLorean…for real! You are a spaceship! You are time-traveling right now! And like Andre 3000 eloquently laid out to us, "spaceships don't come equipped with rearview mirrors, they dip!"

We are not meaningless. **YOUR LIFE IS NOT INSIGNIFICANT.** *It's the opposite! You just being alive* **IS A VEHICLE THAT GOD IS USING SPECIFICALLY FOR HIS PURPOSES.**

So how do we "dip" in our vehicles? We all know that the first definition of *vehicle* is "a means of transportation" like the DeLorean, but the second definition is "a thing used to express, embody, or fulfill something." Yeah so now we get a little deeper. Let's break that apart.

So we are *a thing* that God created and we were created specifically *to express, embody or fulfill something.* Or, as Paul said in Romans, we are God's manifestation of His "invisible" attributes. Just like the vast, endless sky and the deep unexplorable oceans, we are God's visible and tangible manifestation of His "invisible qualities." I hope this shines some light on the much debated line in Genesis about being "created in God's own image."

What does this mean for your everyday life? How can this help us in the challenges and problems and issues we have right now? Paul is telling us that our creator expresses His power through our lives, just like He does through mountains, waterfalls, or eclipses and sunsets. So, the same force that created the Cosmos and all of the stars, planets and black holes, also woke you up this morning! The same force that blows tornadoes, hurricanes and tsunamis also gave you the breath you just took. Look, you are not just experiencing life. Trust me; you are NOT "just living." You ARE life. When God had a thought, your life happened. Don't leave that thought unfulfilled.

Even an evolutionist still understands that our bodies are literally made from mud, being animated by a life force, and those bodies all return to mud once the animation ends. There is no difference between my hand when it digs into the soil and the soil itself, other than the invisible power of God manifesting through me like we talked about earlier. *That* force that animates us—making us living souls—is not GIVING us life, it IS life in itself and of itself. So "you," regardless of your personality, regardless of whatever name you like to call yourself, regardless of what you have been through, what you really are is a life force inside of a physical body that is temporarily here to do some work. Don't forget who you are.

God's Toolbox

In the garden of Gethsemane when Jesus was preparing to surrender to His death, He prayed and asked God to remove this fate from Him. He ended that same prayer by saying that 'God's will' would be done and not His personal wishes. He accepted His purpose, as painful and scary as it was. Accepting our own purpose is the example Jesus set that day in the garden.

The story shows that even Jesus had an assignment that was different than what He would have preferred. In that moment of fear and anxiety, He showed obedience not only to God, but to His specific purpose. He knew He was a sacrifice. He was a lamb. When you really think about it, we all are. I don't care who you are, how successful you get to be, you only get a certain number of years here. That life you treasure is temporary and will be a sacrifice to the glory of something when you are done. The only question is, What will get the glory? What will your life glorify? See, life will be full of struggles, but if we manage to drive in our actual purpose, the results of our work are magnified by God's power, so that there are no limits to what your life can mean to the world if in the end He gets the glory.

That life you treasure is temporary and will be a sacrifice to the GLORY OF SOMETHING WHEN YOU ARE DONE. THE ONLY QUESTION *is, What will* GET THE GLORY?

For God's purpose, Jesus was a lamb—a blood sacrifice in an ancient time. What are you meant to be for God's purpose? You can be a useful tool in God's hands.

My father was forty-nine years older than me and he was raised in rural Alabama on a forty-acre farm. Being two generations younger and from a completely different upbringing than my father means that some of my earliest memories are of me taking note at exactly how different we were physically. As I would ride in the passenger seat of his pickup truck, I would sneak looks at him out of the corner of my eye. I would see the wrinkles of his face, the muscles of his arms and, most of all, I would stare at his hands. I remember his hands being so calloused and strong and, when he would shake mine, his hands gave me a feeling of sandpaper—very rough. Half a century of hard manual labor had not just made his hands rough, but they had even become shaped differently. They were shaped almost like tools. Essentially they *were* tools. To adapt to all that manual work, his hands had taken on the most useful physical properties for their purpose. His hands had accepted what they were meant for. Everything that I have ever learned about purpose was metaphorically summed up in my father's hands. My father had allowed his entire body to be a tool as he built houses for people who needed a place to stay, and served those less fortunate. If I had to compare him to something we can all relate to, he would be something like a John Deere or a multi-tool from Home Depot.

I had a conversation with my wife recently and we started trying to figure out what kind of tools we were in "God's toolbox." We don't do manual farm labor, so it's not so easy to tell through our hands. After talking through it, we decided that she was a flashlight. She shoots straight and direct and is always focused on uncovering truth. In all aspects of her life, these same qualities tend to come out. We also decided that I'm a microphone. I take words and thoughts and amplify them to crowds. Even when I'm talking in one-on-one convo, I amplify my words and speak with passion...like I'm trying to penetrate through to the person's heart and soul—which I am. Looking at it in that way lets us visualize our purpose and makes obedience take on a new light.

When I get called to speak in front of crowds of people and I start getting nervous or feeling anxiety about what I need to do, I just remind myself right in that moment, "Jay, you are designed to do this. You *have to* do it. The people in the room have been placed here to hear what you will say." It's my role. Like an actual vehicle, it's my make and model. Should a crane or a steamroller be anxious about arriving for duty at a construction site? I'm not saying I'm perfect or better than everybody else at anything, but I am saying that even if I struggle, I'm meant to be the one struggling in that moment.

My wife and I looking at ourselves as a "flashlight" and "microphone" also gave us some insight into some areas where we may be vulnerable or have blind spots. A microphone can amplify messages to the masses but would be crazy awkward when used in face-to-face conversations. In other words, there are times where a more practical approach is needed, such that trying to penetrate someone's heart and soul is counterproductive in the moment. So, I need to learn to adjust to the moments when I need to stay and address what's on the surface. In the same way, a flashlight may focus its light so directly and narrow scope that it can overlook things on the periphery. In other words, my wife has to watch for overlooking collateral damage outside of emotions that may be outside her focus. So identifying how we are designed means identifying our strengths and weaknesses. As a couple, God has balanced us so we learn to cover each other, but it starts with growth at the individual level with God. It's important to note that, not all growth towards purpose happens slowly. You may be delivered and challenged with stepping into your purpose as soon as tomorrow. Embrace the discomfort of being pulled.

Hit the gas! What you CAN change right now:

1. Set your cell phone alarm to go off 30 minutes earlier tomorrow and rename the alarm "Today is a new Benz...drive it."
2. Find a way to do ONE THING this week that exhibits the type of instrument you are. Ex. if you are a _____, then go out and _____.

Chapter 2

The Back Seat

"Therefore to him that knoweth to do good, and doeth it not, to him this is a sin." (James 4:17)

How Did I Get Stuck in the Back Seat?

In the winter of 2008, after a breakup in a relationship, I went to see a therapist. Yeah, black men do go to therapists...sometimes. This was before I had ever written any books, taught any life groups or done any speeches. In fact, it was during a period of my life where I struggled hardcore with depression and anxiety. When I was in that dark period, I hardly ever discussed anything I was dealing with in my personal life with anybody, not even my closest friends. I was embarrassed at the fact I was struggling emotionally, and I felt like if I told people, it would make them see me as some kind of weird person to be pitied, like a circus freak. In my mind, I felt that if I opened up and shared what I was going through, my own friends would look at me differently. They would look at me the way that you look at people who had been maimed or disfigured in some accident or born with a deformity. "My life is deformed" is what I told myself. I hadn't visited any church or thought about any kind of intentional walk with God, so

I had a lot of painful things bottled up inside me and no feasible route out of it.

The therapist that I visited got the first glimpse into what would soon become my personal testimony and the basis of my life coaching. The first visit, I sat on her couch and spoke uninterrupted for at least an hour. I relived the stories of my life and painted her a picture of the memories of my family members that I would later write into my first book. The pain of losing so many loved ones was finally exhaled into actual words. I had walked into that lady's office and dumped out a million-piece jigsaw puzzle right there on the floor and started solving it. During that session, I told her a story where I described the way that I had learned most of what I knew about life. Here is what I described to her:

> I had learned many of my life lessons by sitting in the backseat of our family car and leaning forward through the middle of the two front seats and absorbing all the dialog of my mom and my older brother. The years of my early childhood were rough. I would realize later that this was the period when my parents were getting divorced. The three of us found ourselves driving around in our car and eating a ton of fast food. I would poke my head up into the front seat and basically "go to school" by listening to my mom and brother talk about everything under the sun. They were two of the most intelligent and curious people I would ever meet, so I was doing pretty good with them as my touchstones. I learned complicated words, concepts, ideas and philosophies right there inside

that moving vehicle. My brain would race to keep up and process everything. It was a crash course in life that would one day actually crash for me. When I was sixteen, and he nineteen, my brother was killed by gun violence.

After what seemed like hours of rambling to my therapist about my life, she finally had her turn to speak. She was surprisingly entertained with my stories and enamored with my strength. She said that I had been able to maintain remarkable stability given the circumstances and gave me kudos on having the self-awareness to know that therapy was a needed step. When it came time to give me notes on where I was now and what I should work on, her summation was this: I had stunted my growth by not properly mourning my mom and brother and I was psychologically and spiritually still "in that backseat." My experiences with them had been the foundation of my early life and education, but now that the two drivers were gone, I was still coasting along, allowing my life to collide full speed into whatever flew in its path. I was crashing, literally, and simply numbing the pain by curling up and hiding even deeper in the back seat.

Her prescription was this: I ought to properly mourn the deaths of my mother and brother so I can then move from the back seat and into the driver's seat of my life. In other words, stop letting life happen to me, and learn how to let it happen through me.

Whoa. The light went off for me. I looked back at all my life turmoil and knew that she was right. I really *had* been in that back seat letting life just happen to me, crashing into things.

After my brother died, I really settled into the backseat. In all aspects of my life, I just went through the motions. At school, my grades went from excellent to horrible and I never regained the passion for school, which I once had. My teachers at school showed a ton of concern, but I was so emotionally unavailable that I couldn't bring myself to do any better.

THE BACKSEAT IS A PLACE OF PASSIVE-AGGRESSIVE BEHAVIOR.

Five years later, when my mother died of a heart attack after never being able to cope with my brother's death, that blow really sealed me into the back seat. In public, I maintained a front that kept everybody away from knowing my inner turmoil. I felt that everybody probably looked at me like "the guy whose whole family died," so I became more and more socially awkward. In relationships, I refused to form any bonds that would be deep enough to hurt me in the way that losing my brother and mom had. So I flailed and failed with relationships, jobs and friendships because I was unable to give back any of the attachment I was receiving. I hurt a lot of people in the process. I was a complete zombie. In my mind, life was happening *to* me and I couldn't stop it. Because I was still holding on to the pain from those deaths in my past, I figured I wasn't meant to enjoy much of life anyway, so I just played along, mostly suffering. I worked jobs that came easy to me. I dated girls that felt safe for me or, at least, seemed just as damaged as I was. I spent my time in things that were not likely to challenge me or shake my comfort zone. I pursued an underground music career that had the cards stacked against it from the start. I never mustered the courage to really commit enough of myself to any of those jobs, women or passions to overcome the odds. I had pretty much built a fortress for my own depression. I had pimped out the back seat.

The backseat is a place of passive-aggressive behavior. Just imagine going out to your car to go to work in the morning and instead of driving there, just sitting in the backseat and waiting for the place you work to miraculously come to you. That sounds crazy, but this is what I did in my life. This is what you could be doing right now if you don't make the needed changes.

Remember, it's your life...it's your Benz with the bow on it sitting in the driveway gleaming. Get in and drive. Don't just hop in the back seat and wait. Don't wait for your career to drive to you. Don't wait on your purpose to spell itself out on the windows you are fogging up while scrolling through IG or Snapchat at people who seem to be doing so much more than you are. Look up front at that key in the ignition and ask God for the courage to drive closer to Him.

In the first chapter of this book, I compared life to Marty McFly's car from the *Back to the Future* movie. That DeLorean did some spectacular stuff once it got super-charged by an external power force. We won't do anything significant either unless we are tapped in to the supernatural

23

power force that created us. But, just like when Marty drove that bad boy to the clock tower at the perfect time to get the power of the lightning bolt, we also need to start moving in our life to get from where we are now to the place, job, and/or mind state at the right time so we can best access the power source. We need to get to our clock tower.

To get there, you have to get out of the confines of the backseat. For me, that meant mourning my loved ones; for you, that could mean something very different. Prepare yourself to do that hard work. Take a deep breath right now and seriously challenge yourself to answer the following list of yes/no questions. Remember, instead of forming an answer right away, consider what a 'yes' and a 'no' really means for you. Really wrap your brain around what each answer looks like on you. Let's go:

> Q: Do I avoid the discomfort of interacting with the very people who could be sent specifically to help me along my path?
> Q: Do I push away new and potentially healthy people who come into my life?
> Q: Do I turn down invitations to church services or group gatherings because of my feelings of how flawed "church folk" are?

Q: Do I refuse to do things with my free time that are outside of the comfort zone stuff I'm already used to?

Q: Do I refuse to be challenged in my opinions or stances on something?

Q: Have I dated someone and found a way to sabotage the relationship when they seemed like a person that expected a lot from me?

Q: Do I spend a frustrating amount of my free time pursuing things that bring me little success and/or fulfillment?

Q: Have I felt nervous when approached with a new opportunity and bailed out so that I don't have to deal with the anxiety?

Q: Do I hate my current job and feel lost on what to do next?

Take a second to process how you feel about your answers.

Look, we all have scars. We all have been hurt in our past and, trust me, we will be hurt again in our futures. But these new scars...are they going to be *defensive* wounds or *offensive* wounds? I mean, pain happens no matter what. You will still experience hurt while sitting back in your comfort zone and trying to block the blows, so you might as well bring the fight to life. It makes more sense to suffer pain while on a mission, than never start any mission and still suffer pain. I believe you want the offensive wounds. I think you're done sitting and waiting on your purpose to drive up to you. You want to live in your purpose right now. So let's start driving.

Find the Seatbelt

The first step in becoming an active driver of your life is to identify the things in your past that are keeping you strapped in the backseat. I call this *finding the seatbelt*. This is by far the most difficult work to get started on and, to be honest, most people will need some help to complete this step. As a life coach, 90% of my counseling is done in this area. It may be tough, but it is vital, and there is no shame in looking for another person, be it a friend, accountability partner, life coach, therapist, etc. to help you out.

The reason it's so hard to find the seatbelt is that, by nature, you have kept most of the root causes hidden even from yourself. How can you find something that you purposely hid? Your childhood probably has at least a few gaps and blurry memories that are too painful to process. The problem is, those things are keeping you tied to the emotions of those moments and holding you back from growing past them and developing. After so many years of being hidden and allowed to fester in a dark corner, all those memorized emotions become strapped to our backs, weighing us down. Imagine trying to run a marathon with a rope tied to your waist and iron weights attached to the rope.

Once you decide to turn around and face your past, you can begin the work of digging through the dark stuff and finding those things that are acting as your seatbelt. This calls for you to get your courage up, get your armor for battle (Bible, prayer, accountability partner, life coach), and to march back into the memory of the day you were abused, or got diagnosed with a sickness, or (as it was for me) found out somebody you love has passed away and start cutting those rope. No matter how bad it is or how long you've held on to it, there is healing waiting for you. You just have to be the one willing to do the work to go get it. No one can give it to you.

We may even find that what's holding us in the backseat is more of a booster or child seat. Some of these weights date all the way back to when we were infants, when we were most vulnerable and needing extra protection from the dangers of the drive, and did not get all that we needed.

Open the Door

Yeah, I know, "open the door" sounds simple, but it is everything. The door represents our defense mechanisms that we think have been protecting us from the dangers of the outside world. Opening up represents courage. It takes courage to let down your guard. If you want to be a driver, you have no choice. We are adults now and no longer children in the backseat. Step out into the air and breathe. Do this; wherever you are right now, stand up and look all around you. Stretch your legs. Walk around in a small circle. Let the blood circulate throughout your entire framework. Let the fresh air invigorate you. Close your eyes. Envision the places you can and will go and imagine yourself driving there. Imagine yourself reaching down and grabbing the driver's seat door.

You will probably find that it is locked...from the inside. For many of us, the hidden dark moments are so unhealthy and overgrown that they become mental health issues. This was the case for me. After going to see a therapist and explaining the traumas from my childhood, I was diagnosed with Post Traumatic Stress Disorder and Panic Disorder. Both of those disorders involve anxiety and both make it difficult for me to interact with people in the ways I need to. But, both are only weaknesses of the flesh. I am able to overcome these disorders because the same God that created the Sun, Moon and rest of the Cosmos also manifested my life, so no physical shortcoming is strong enough to hold back the full thought God had when I was created. The creator also created you to do something. If you seek Him, nothing can stand in the way of your future.

Now, open the door and get out of your backseat.

Hit the gas! What you can change right now:

1. Make a list of all the reasons why you can't take control of your life right now.
2. Go down the list and for each reason, write down somebody you know of that has overcome that hurdle. Think real hard about it. If you can name one person that has overcome each hurdle that you are stuck in, then your reason for staying stuck is not what you think it is. The issue doesn't lie in your inability but in your fear.

Chapter 3

Drive!

> "Having then gifts differing according to the grace that is given to us, *let us use them:* if prophecy, *let us prophesy* in proportion to our faith; or ministry, *let us use it* in *our* ministering; he who teaches, in teaching; he who exhorts, in exhortation; he who gives, with liberality; he who leads, with diligence; he who shows mercy, with cheerfulness." (Romans 12:6-8)

Driver's Ed

The moment you hop in that driver's seat, the first thing you will notice is that this vehicle ain't your ordinary vehicle. This is *not* a car. There is no simple gear shift to just pop it into drive and go. These gears are all over the place. The dashboard is complex and hard to read. Some of the warning lights might even be flashing little shapes at us that we can't understand. Because we've sat in the backseat for so long, the vehicle might not even be in great driving shape. We might find ourselves sitting behind the wheel scared to death, no different than a teenager about to hop on the road for the first time.

The reality is, we are that teenager and this is scary work. Hopping out on that road means we have to navigate some dangerous situations. It means that even though we might

But despite what might have been lacking inside our house, God **STILL EMPOWERS US TO GO AND FIND WHAT WE NEED**

try to be cautious and thoughtful out there, the other drivers won't always be. There are no guarantees about what anybody else is going through and their own maturity and pain. We have to keep up with the speed of traffic no matter how fast life is going and there won't always be a

soft shoulder to pull over on. So we need a little bit of Driver's Ed. By that I mean, going out and *learning* how to drive in life, even if it means we have to go find somebody more experienced who can walk us through it. We need somebody who can help us figure out the basics of how we should best drive this "vehicle." What is our gas pedal—or should I say—what is it that fuels or motivates us? Where is the brake pedal—or what could trigger me to slow down or even freeze? What is the thing that can threaten to shift us into reverse?

We live in a fallen world, so none of us are going to be born into flawless situations. None of us were raised by parents with no flaws, who showed us flawless examples of unconditional love and never allowed any harm to come to us. Nah. Life didn't work that way for any of us. But despite what might have been lacking inside our house, God still empowers us to go and find what we need. All of what we need is here, if we are willing to be guided towards it.

For example, if you don't live in an environment that's spiritually fertile, where healthy situations and people exist all around you, you just might have to move to place yourself where healthy situations do exist. You might even have to learn how to "farm" them yourself. Let's say you are part of a family or grew up in a neighborhood with literally no positive role models. Maybe your father figures all got locked up and their behavior has been normalized to the prison system. Maybe your mother figures were scarred emotionally and doing the job of two parents. In both situations, they may love you but also lack exposure to healthy ways of showing that love. Maybe both situations are true for you, and they intersect to make both problems even worse.

If you humble yourself and ask God for His eyes, He will make obvious to you the numerous people (football coach or guidance counselor or dude who came to your school on career day dressed like a herb) that have already been placed around you (cheerleading coach, a friend's parent, or career day lady from that business downtown), ready to fill the gap in the areas your own upbringing came up short. God is always working for the good of those who seek Him and are called according to His purposes. So, first, seek Him by asking for His eyes to see more of His plan. Then follow His call, which may lead you somewhere you are not familiar. Doing this, you will find that there is no shortage of people placed there to give you lessons on how to drive this thing called life.

The bottom line is that the fact that something you need doesn't naturally grow near you simply means you need to go find it. My father used to say "Lobsters don't exist in Lake Erie but you all can enjoy some for dinner here in Cleveland, Ohio...why? Because you want them and are willing to pay to have it." We just have to want healthy people in our life just as bad as we all like good seafood! We have to be willing to pay, or go above and beyond...maybe even *drive* to get it.

Maybe, for you, you are already past the school phase. Maybe those days flew by you and now you can look back on your life and see how things would have worked out better if somebody *had* spoken to you while you were in school. If that's true, then right now you have the opportunity to close that loop. You have the chance to go speak to some kids who are sitting at their desk the way you used to be and help make sure those kids have a more fertile environment around them. You have a chance to *be* the actual kind of person you once needed.

Know Your Engine

I want to be clear that when I talk about getting up and getting out of the backseat and driving your life, I absolutely do not expect for that kind of action and energy to just come naturally and easily to all of you. Everybody is wired differently and we all approach life with a different natural energy. Science and psychology tend to categorize personalities as either an Alpha (self-assured and outgoing), a Beta (moderate and collaborative), or an Omega (laid back and eccentric). Obviously, not everybody can have an Alpha personality, so not everybody will just jump up excited and eager to tackle every situation in life. That kind of engine is only in some people.

I'm not an Alpha either. When I wake up, my natural qualities are exactly like the description of an Omega. But because I have a desire to see my life play out according to God's plan, so I have decided to adapt to drive like an Alpha when I need to be. You know how you can take an ordinary car and whip that bad boy on the highway sometimes and keep up with the German-engineered cars that cost five times what yours did and have far more horsepower than yours? Yeah, just like that. God can take your focus and determination and give you the right timing and anticipation to make you drive in any lane HE needs you in, no matter what motor you have. So, the priority you place on using your God-given gifts to best fulfill the promise of your "vehicle" or "thing that God made" can super-charge the natural energy that you wake up with. Just like Marty's DeLorean; your drive towards your purpose can be just as strong of a fuel as what an "Alpha Dog" wakes up with, if you let Christ magnify it.

The difference is that if it doesn't burn naturally for you, then you have to know that and make adjustments. Build the Flux Capacitor and hook that wire up to the clock tower. If you know you don't have that fire in your gut when you wake up every morning, then you have to wake up and pray for help and build some effective rituals and routines that reignite that intensity every day and keep that engine blazing.

Routine Maintenance

The legendary sci-fi author Octavia Butler once said this about the benefit of relying on habits over inspiration:

> "First, forget inspiration. Habit is more dependable. Habit will sustain you whether you're inspired or not. Habit will help you finish and polish your stories. Inspiration won't. Habit is persistence in practice."

What you usually think of inspiration can be largely affected by mood. Your mood is driven by our emotions. Emotions are untrustworthy. They are literally the effect of chemicals flowing through your brain that change in unreliable ways. You cannot afford to leave the day-to-day operations of your drive towards purpose entirely, or even mainly, up to your emotions. You need to have a solid foundation that keeps you grounded, especially in the morning when our mood is especially vulnerable. The moment you wake up, your mood is looking to shift. Those chemicals in your brain have been settled while you were sleep and your brain immediately starts blasting out chemicals as soon as you wake up. The problem is, our basic animal instinct wants to prepare against threats like lions and bears. We don't usually have those direct threats so it replaces those fears with irrational ones. If there is anything negative around, your mood will be fueled by it, and your engine can be affected. This is why people who suffer from anxiety-related issues (like myself) have seen our biggest struggles occur first thing in the morning. The negative thoughts creep in instantly as we wake up and trigger a flood of hormones that set a bad tone for the day.

Let's talk about some routines you can implement to add horsepower to your natural engine:

- Read something every day.

    It doesn't matter if it's the back of the air freshener canister when you are using the bathroom, just read something *that is non-fiction* every single day. Your brain is a muscle. It can only respond well to new things if you keep it sharp and ready.

- Improve your communication.

  No matter whether it's via email, text, or face-to-face chats, we all can definitely work to improve how we communicate. To do that: first, eliminate passive-aggressive behavior and words. Before you send something out, or ignore an incoming call or act like you don't see somebody standing ten feet away, ask yourself "...am I doing this the stand-up way or am I bailing out somehow? Am I looking at my own accountability in this or am I really trying to replace the best action with this one?" These types of improvements take time so you have to think about it every chance you can.

- Start the day positive.

  If you allow negativity during your mornings, you will start your day behind the 8-ball and have to make up ground to make progress in your purpose. Allowing these types of mood swings makes it even harder to keep the routines we talked about a couple bullet points up. To avoid this instant crash of emotion, build in some guardrails. Place tools around you that fight the negative thoughts. Do something that kick-starts your day in the direction you predetermine in your walk with God. Our cell phones are the first thing we check, so instead of trying to avoid it, empower it! Instead of it being a rabbit hole into things you don't want your mind on, make it a gateway to what you *do* want to see. Install a Bible app and read the verse of the day (to go deeper, dig into the whole chapter) as soon as you wake up. Trim your social media lists to show you positive vibes instead of negative ones. Even install an app filter or simply uninstall the apps that show the most negative images and replace them with healthier ones.

- Take care of your health

  This is not a health food or nutrition book, but one of the most important factors to keeping your engine running at high efficiency is to stay as healthy as you can. The difference between an Alpha to a Beta or Omega personality, keeping up with the Alphas can sometimes be that the body isn't running at its best. You might have a vitamin deficiency. For example, having a Vitamin D deficiency can cause moodiness, especially in mornings. Take a yearly physical and find out if you have something along those lines and do the work to supplement your body where it is in need. Don't blow your opportunities by waking up late for your first day at work or being "hangry" in a meeting when it could have been avoided. Don't waste your gift over a vitamin deficiency, y'all.

Hit the gas! What you CAN change right now:

1. Find the one thing that's giving you the most anxiety right now and the very next time it comes

up, whether it's a conversation that you have to have or a decision you have to make or a situation that seems out of your control, whatever it is, when it comes up, TAKE AN ACTIVE STAND. Use an ACTIVE VOICE. Kill the passive aggressiveness in your life RIGHT NOW.

2. Implement a routine starting TONIGHT. You're reading this book, so the first step is done. Now follow up tomorrow and keep going. No matter whether you are a natural Alpha personality or not, let your regimen fuel you like one.

3. Schedule a yearly physical.

Chapter 4

The Rubber Meets the Road

> God says, "Rebuild the road! Clear away the rocks
> and stones so my people can return from captivity."
> (Isaiah 57:14 NLT)

Once you start driving in your life, you will start to see transformation in who you are. Your habits will change. The old version of you did things a certain way, but now you are holding the steering wheel with the ability to correct those old paths. And that's exactly what your next step should be.

Repairing Old Roads

When I use the term "driving your life," I am talking about taking an active role in your situations. You are no longer a wallflower at the party of life, you get out there dancing, offbeat or not! The challenge is that since you haven't been living like this, then once you do start, you will notice the roads you are driving your new red-bow "vehicle" on are torn up from your old passive-aggressive actions. You will find that your communication channels are awkward now because you spent so much time being passive-aggressive with your words before. You find that your habits are not trustworthy because of the many times you tried to dodge responsibility by getting defensive instead of owning up to your faults. You will find that the people around you, either in our families or at work, have grown to *expect* you to be passive and they interact with you prepared for a possible bad experience. It can and will be awkward to interact with them without giving them the old you that they have grown to expect. Believe in yourself and your new direction, you have the strength to overcome the awkwardness.

When you start looking at the roads that you have built this whole time, you may find that many of them need repair. If you are anything like me (and you probably are), and you used to lie and run from responsibility the way I used to, then those roads are pretty jacked up and full of potholes. Some of them might just be completely unpaved! Just straight dirt. If you do find that you stayed in that backseat too long and floated into delayed adolescence, then a lot of your relationships were probably built without using any good tools. So, now you have these roads surrounding us in our life that were built from years of poor communication, lack of accountability, and passive-aggressive habits. Imagine a whole city completely in disrepair, that's what you have created. And many of the people in that city have been hurt by you and don't trust your actions, your word, or your intentions. To keep it 100, you are essentially like a bad politician—full of lies, empty promises, and blame game. You are the Mayor of this broken down town. Your job is to do something about it.

A good place to start is by making amends for the things you did wrong to the people you hurt. Trust me, I know, this part sucks. But the problem is, it's impossible to drive on to another town with healthier roads when we still have unresolved damage surrounding our current situations. Look, the people we hurt may never like us again, love us again or forgive us for what we did, so these might be roads that we never drive on again in life. Even in those cases, we can at least make the effort to leave a patch in the bad road as you drive away.

Exploring New Traffic

Along with building better roads comes the opportunity for you to start driving into new areas, exploring new neighborhoods and mingling in different traffic. You will find yourself around the people that make up the fertile ground for you to grow in your purpose. The crowd around you will change, not necessarily in a way of being with "better" people, either. It's not a matter of better and worse. You will simply be led to be around the people you are meant to affect through your purpose and also who affect you through theirs.

One comment, when **IN THE PRESENCE OF THOSE WHO YOU** *are meant to affect, can literally change* **THE WORLD.**

Back in my mid-twenties, I dove head first into doing music. I gravitated towards a group of artists in upstate New York. I found myself driving out there week after week to record and hang with this collective of emcees, DJs, and producers, enjoying each other's culture and intelligence; and together, we built our own record label. One day, while we were all at a bar just bonding and kicking it, one of the friends said, "Yo, don't chase your liquor, chase your dreams, man." The conviction on his face reflected more than just drunk, slurred bravado. There was something deeper. We could all tell that he was *meant* to say that to us. We laughed way longer than expected for a small comment like that and we told the story of that night a lot over the years. I noticed that as I moved on in life into new ventures and uncharted territory, that night and that quote always come rushing back to me. I even have a plaque on my office wall at home sitting right behind me now that says "chase your dreams." I use the idea and story often when I'm mentoring clients as a life coach, in motivational speeches, and (obviously) in my books. So, just through me, that one moment has touched thousands. Who knows how far those words have traveled on the tongues of the other people at that bar that night. Who knows where they have all been and what they have all achieved.

I say all that so you can realize that, when you find yourself around the people you are meant to affect, all you have to do is say one small comment and it can travel miles and transcend time and cultures. One comment, when in the presence of those who you are *meant* to affect, can literally change the world.

Hit the gas! What you CAN change right now:

1. Examine the roads you are driving on right now. Identify ONE "pothole road" in your daily life— that is, one thing where you can admit you have passive-aggressive behavior or words.
2. Make the decision today to patch that pothole. Reach out and make amends, or at the very least, fill the hole with your new behavior. If it's awkward, then you're probably doing it right.

Chapter 5

It's the Journey, not the Destination

> "Forget the former things; do not dwell on the
> past. See, I am doing a new thing! Now it springs
> up; do you not perceive it? I am making a way in
> the wilderness and streams in the wasteland."
> (Isaiah 43:18-19)

In 1981, the band Journey made the hit song "Don't Stop
Believing." That's the only thing I know about the band,
but that's enough. The fact that a band named Journey sang
a timeless song called "Don't Stop Believing" is too good
of a connection for me not to discuss in this book. Once
you learn how to grab the wheel and start occupying the
driver's seat of your life, the real journey begins…so don't
stop believing now!

Course Correction

I got baptized for the first time at the ripe old age of thirty-
seven. The ceremony was symbolic of the death of my old

self and the birth of a new self in Christ. The moment my head came back up from the water, I had received God's special grace and had been redeemed, but it was still my responsibility to do the work needed to stay on course. I had to get ready to obey God's course correction. This is what you will face now that you have started driving.

Every time I try to type on my phone and use the letter 'u' instead of typing out the entire word 'you,' my phone corrects it to 'I'. Crazy and annoying, right? It frustrates me and I am tempted to remove that autocorrect feature, but I know in a strange way it's only happening in order to make me a better communicator. So after several times of doing this and getting frustrated, I had to think to myself, "I'm forty years old, why am I typing 'u' instead of 'you'?" I know it's cool to be casual sometimes but overall, it should be the exception to the rule to take that kind of shortcut. So, if that's what I choose to do as an exception to the rule, then the autocorrect issue is something that's not a problem, it's just a guardrail to keep me on my toes for the majority of my communication. It's a perspective shift.

I can recall a story I heard from a CEO I once worked for. He told a room full of employees a story about how airplanes fly. They do not, he said, fly in a straight line. Instead, along the flight, their course is constantly corrected by a navigation system that senses how far off the planned path the plane is at regular time intervals. In the end, if you could visibly chart the path the plane has taken from departure to destination, it would actually be a long and erratic zigzag pattern, not a straight line from point A to point B.

Well, our lives are navigated the same way. The only straight path you or I could ever accomplish alone is straight to disaster. When we drive, we absolutely require course correction. God gives His course correction, leading us by divine intervention, through the people we meet and situations we are put in. The more in tune we are with the His plan for us, and the more we choose to obey His call, the closer we come to our purpose. Listen closely to the corrections occurring around you right now. You probably find most of them as annoying as my phone autocorrect. Pray and ask for discernment and listen again. We are usually just ignoring the correction that we don't want to receive.

Here is something I've been trying to let soak into my soul, my habits and my thoughts. All of the things, people and situations that we *don't* like are actually happening for a reason. That reason is to build and sharpen us for the purpose that God has for our lives. In life, we are continually pulled away from the comfort zone of who we think we are and all of the elaborate self-protection we have crafted to keep up the facade. Check this scripture:

"My son, do not despise the chastening of the Lord , Nor detest His correction; For whom the Lord loves He corrects, Just as a father the son in whom he delights. Happy is the man who finds wisdom, And the man who gains understanding." (Proverbs 3:11-13 NKJV)

Go back to your Bible or Bible app and bookmark this one. Use this as a reminder to not be annoyed at correction. Here is a tip: If during the day you find yourself complaining out loud about something or not being able to do something, flip the logic on its head and see how the answer May lie in something you can do better. Ask yourself, "If I change so that this is not a complaint anymore, am I better for it?" Many times, the answer is "Absolutely."

Our Daddy's Business

There are plenty of days where I take my kids out of the house to run errands with me. On these trips, my kids are not aware at all of how many places we have to go or where these places are. They don't know how long we are going to be gone or the purpose and importance of each stop. I will definitely have to keep reminding them over and over of why we are out and it will seem like I'm speaking a whole different language because they seem to forget as soon as I

48

tell them. Over the course of the whole thing, they might complain and start whining or they might surprise me and show patience, but one thing I know for sure is they definitely have other things they would rather want to be doing! If it was up to them, we would be off doing something for their juvenile entertainment, like going to a toy store or a playground. If they were leading they would run, laugh and play and none of the vital business I need to handle will get done.

Well, don't we, as adults, do that same thing? We get led off on these journeys in life and have no idea how far they will take us or how long they will last. We don't quite understand the real importance of each stop. We need constant reminders of what the trip really is about. Left up to us, we would be doing something else. In fact, many of us *are* doing something else and have left our real purpose on hold. Are you metaphorically off in the toy store or on the merry-go-round in the middle of the mall while you should be handling our Father's business? Are you running, laughing and playing? What about the "vital business" that the Father has for you? Will you go with Him, without whining and complaining? Will you accept His timing?

You know how people who work in cubicles or offices tend to post pictures of their family all around them? When I was younger and before I had a family, I used to think that was corny. I had no concept of why they would do it. Now

I understand. Most people don't absolutely love their job. They are there, in a cubicle, putting up with a ton of crap for the entire day. They get to work, they leave and they probably feel unfulfilled when it's done. But they can look up at their family and know what motivates them to keep going. This is how we have to also learn to approach living in our purpose. It may be different than the life we had planned for ourselves. It is definitely going to be challenging, but we have to stay focused on why we do it and who we are looking to please by doing it. So the more ways you can find to focus on your "cubicle picture" motivation, the more we stay engaged in the mission despite the grueling hours and sacrifice. The payday will be glorious.

Road Trips

As a car driver, road trips can be some of the most trying experiences of our lives, but they also build memories with our loved ones, driving stamina and skills that we could not get any other way. The same benefits apply when "driving our lives."

In the classic Disney/Pixar movie *"Finding Nemo,"* I love the character Marlin because he has so many realistically human behavior traits. In the story, Marlin is the father of the title character, Nemo. Just as we are introduced to this new family of clownfish, Marlin experiences the loss of everything that is dear to him. He loses his children and wife to a shark attack. Then, while moving on through life showing the classic signs of post-traumatic stress syndrome, he then loses his only surviving son to the ocean. Deciding to finally stop letting life happen to him, he decides to hop in the Driver's Seat and swims across the entire ocean to find his son. Along the way, the characters sent to help him on this journey are all people that he finds truly unpleasant and annoying. They all have the perfect storm of quirks to drive him absolutely up a wall, so his dedication to the journey is definitely tested. We ultimately see, though, that those characters also have exactly the combination of qualities to help him get where he needs to go. In this popular kids' movie, we see a picture of how God works in our lives and gives us what we need to fulfill our destinies. We even get to see that Marlin's name is elevated in throughout the journey as his courageous story spreads throughout the ocean.

Like Marlin, all of the people you have met along the way have left you with tools and pieces of knowledge on how to use the tools to get things fixed when you get stuck. And if we really get stuck out there and we need that Good Samaritan, well, that story wasn't told for no reason at all. Those types of people absolutely do show up in our lives right when we need them. The key is discernment and trust. They seem like opposite ideas but they truly work together.

One time last year, my tire exploded while I was driving home on the highway...at night...in the freezing cold...in a bad neighborhood. I drove to the nearest gas station and popped my trunk, expecting to grab the spare tire out of my recently purchased, kinda new, used car. When I looked inside the trunk and opened the tire compartment, it was empty. Instead of a nice un-flat tire, or even a helpful temporary donut, there was just a jack, a small power generator and an electric air pump with flat-fixing spray in it. I had forgotten to look through the car when I bought it to see if it had an actual spare tire. Bad move. I went about trying to use what I had to get

HERE'S THE SECRET. IT HAS TO BE HARD. THE ROAD HAS TO BE TOUGH OR BECAUSE THE VICTORY YOU SEEK IS GREAT.

back going. I grabbed the generator and the flat-fixing electric pump and started trying to make it work. After about 5 minutes of pumping this stuff into my tire, nothing was happening except my hands were starting to freeze to where I couldn't feel or move them. A woman and a man approached me and asked if I needed help. Over the course of the next two hours, they pointed me in the direction of the only place to buy a tire at that time of night. To be honest, I didn't enjoy their personalities or attitudes at all. Just allowing them to help me was unpleasant. I was quite literally Marlin from Finding Nemo. Everything in me wanted to cut my losses, take an Uber home and deal with the situation at a later time with different people. But, instead of pushing back against it and potentially being ungrateful to them, I looked at them for what they were, God's way of giving me exactly what I needed to get back on the road and drive...and an opportunity to improve my patience and tolerance of folks.

Here's the secret. It has to be hard. The road has to be tough or because the victory you seek is great. If your road has been easy, then you have definitely not been after the most worthy goals. As Denzel Washington puts it, "Ease is a greater threat to progress than hardship" or as Jesus' half-brother James puts it in the scripture:

> *My brethren, count it all joy when you fall into various trials, knowing that the testing of your faith produces patience. But let patience have its perfect work, that you may be perfect and complete, lacking nothing. (James 1:2-4)*

To take it even further and add detail to the benefits of putting up with people or situations that annoy us, Paul in the book of Galatians says that the benefits or "Fruit of the Spirit" can actually be listed:

1. Love
2. Joy
3. Peace
4. Patience

5. Kindness
6. Goodness
7. Faithfulness
8. Gentleness
9. Self-control

The crazy thing is, these things are the answer to every prayer we have. These are the solution and keys to our locked doors and tough predicaments. So if we change our habits enough to invest in doing things God's way, we can expect the *payment* to start trickling in, in the form of the actual things we are praying for.

Hit the gas! What you CAN change right now:

1. Identify one person that you have to deal with in an important or frequent way that upsets you or annoys you.
2. Write down all of the "fruits of the Spirit" you could earn by changing your perspective on that person.

Chapter 6

On The Road

"Forget the former things; do not dwell on the past. See, I am doing a new thing! Now it springs up; do you not perceive it? I am making a way in the wilderness and streams in the wasteland." (Isaiah 43:18-19)

Stay Woke!

Now you're driving. You're moving. You are bending corners, testing the speed limits and you got the music knocking and the top down. Now...stay woke! Stay focused because this road is windy and will take some unexpected turns. It's crucial that your eyes stay on the road and that your way is guided by the road map. I know the journey can be long and painstaking. It can take a ton of hard work to rip away those straps that are keeping you stuck in the backseat. It will take a lot of dedication to build new habits to start your engine and drive every day. For some of us, it's going to take years. And the only way to make progress is to stay focused on that road. Don't let yourself be distracted too long! I'm not saying you have to be a robot who can't enjoy the scenery or you can't multitask and steer with your knee for second. I mean, we all do that. You are going to be constantly surrounded by distractions, so you will definitely get caught up in some, but you can't let your eyes focus too long on those traps that take your attention or else you will get lost. And being lost from God's purpose is the darkest place to be. Here are five traps to avoid so we can keep our focus:

- **Ignoring the GPS.** By this, I mean thinking that you can navigate this journey yourself. Thinking that you can make this transition or drive this trip according to our own sense of direction is a recipe for disaster. The old jokes say that men don't ask for directions, but the ugly truth is, both men AND women do this when it comes to spiritual guidance. In fact, we usually want to control the entire journey. First, we procrastinate, not even starting the journey when we *first* are called to. Then once we do get going, we also feel like we are running late, so we start looking for a shortcut. It never pays off. I'm not saying the shortcut won't cut some time, but I am saying that time is not the priority—transformation is. You cannot shortcut the journey God has for you. Every turn is there to build you, every twist is there to establish something in you, and every annoying wait in bumper-to-bumper traffic is designed to make you stronger.

Shortcutting that building process deprives you of strength and leaves you outside of God's will. Think about it, how can we really be *rebuilt* if we keep looking to avoid the *construction*? The true GPS— Greater Power Source—has a route designed just for you. Trust it. Even when you can't find it in you to fully trust it, find the strength to obey just like the child on the errand trip.

• **Visual distractions.** Everywhere you go, people warn you against texting and driving these days. Getting caught up in texting and posting on social media when you are being called to *drive your life* is a problem too. When you started reading this book, you decided to start "driving your life." You did the work to find the things that are keeping you strapped in the backseat of life. You found your way out of them. You found the courage to get out and take the driver's seat. You now have a responsibility not just to yourself, but to those (your family and loved ones) who are relying and dependent on you on the trip. Picture them as passengers in this DeLorean. Going on that kind of journey in life is just like packing your loved ones into a car for a road trip. If you are spending hours on Snapchat, Twitter, Instagram or Facebook, at the same time you're trying to drive, you could be endangering all of your dependents. On another level, if you spend too much time on those same sites before you've even hopped in the driver's seat, that could be exactly what's delaying your calling to start driving. This is no attack on those sites. Some of us find that our lane involves being on those sites and using them as a tool to get further in our journey. Are you using social media to help you drive, or is it a distraction? Are we caught up out here just looking at the world, desiring what's out there instead of doing your own work? Are you caught up staring and lusting at the women or men instead of preparing yourself for the real thing in God's way? Are you focused more on other drivers and other cars than on our own vehicle and the people in it with you? Make sure you stay in your lane.

- **The Rearview Mirror.** Listen, what's behind you should stay behind you. Hopefully, in each of your important past seasons, you can say that you experienced it and received what was meant for you to receive from it. Then drive forward. You can't drive a car by staring in the rearview mirror. Those tests, those trials, those failures, those tears, that pain...they are all behind you. The strength that comes from your past experience only works in your favor if you are not stuck there. Staying focused on someone or something you lost distracts you from all the new replacements God will send. There is a reason that on most vehicles the rearview mirror is small and the front windshield is much larger.

The point of eliminating these distractions is to keep the majority of your focus on your purpose for driving. None of us are going to live forever, so every day we waste is tragic. It's like walking right past that new Benz with the bow on it and taking the bus. The more you allow these types of distractions to invade your daily habits, the longer you will keep "riding the bus," packed in with so many other people, with somebody else driving, and no real destination...just back and forth on the same routes. Don't delay your true journey. The reality is that your vehicle is valuable! None of us are broken-down vehicles on the scrapheap. We are going...full steam ahead. In which direction will you go? The Modern Christian teacher Timothy Keller puts it like this: *"What preoccupies the mind controls the life."*

Are we there yet?

God's path for our life will not look like what we want it to. We are selfish by nature and limited in our knowledge of the universe so when we come up with our own directions, it's always wrong or at least incomplete. Remember, your position to God is no different than children are to the parent when running errands. How patient will you be before you start screaming "are we there yet?"

As you keep driving and you gain some experience, you will start running into some red lights and stop signs. In these moments, you are paused, waiting for further instruction. This is an opportunity to see areas where you can truly transform. If a red light that delays you for 25 seconds in your daily drive to work can actually set off your anger, then most likely your schedule is not set right! You probably woke up late or didn't handle all of your business in the right time, so now you are really just feeling the pressure and conviction from knowing that you could do more. You want a result that you didn't properly prepare to receive. God has been telling you to stop and giving you a change to grow and recognize this. If you wake up on time, you wouldn't have the anxiety of being late. Then the wait at the light wouldn't have the same gravity. You wouldn't be vexed about 25 seconds! Until you accept the lesson contained in the 25-second gift, you are doomed to repeat it and the anger coming after it. So, next time something like this happens to you, try this: instead of getting mad about the light, take the driver's seat in preparation. When you feel that anger rise, let it fuel you to get better instead of aiming it outward. Go home that night and make some changes in how you wake up and get ready. Now the light and 25-second delay have served a purpose to make you better. It's a change agent. You are on Transformation Road.

Hit the gas! What you CAN change right now:

1. Change your social media strategy RIGHT NOW. You've identified earlier what type of tool you can be for God. Decide today that you will not waste time on social media, instead you will use social media to BE the type of God's tool you are designed for. Look back at question #2 at the end of Chapter 1 and remind yourself of what your specific tool was and how you can use your time and energy to be that.

2. Re-read every single post from here out before you click POST and if it does not advance your purpose, delete it.

Epilogue

"Brothers and sisters, I do not consider myself yet to have taken hold of it. But one thing I do: Forgetting what is behind and straining toward what is ahead, I press on toward the goal to win the prize for which God has called me heavenward in Christ Jesus." (Philippians 3:13-14)

Hollywood recently paid homage to the life of a woman named Henrietta Lacks. Mrs. Lacks was a lively, adventurous woman who was diagnosed with cervical cancer back in the early 20th century. Being a poor woman of color in the south at that time, she obviously had many things working against her in winning a battle with cancer. Over the course of her last years, she was inhumanely experimented on and not given the best care and treatment. She lost her battle with the disease. After her death, however, her cells took on a life of their own. Scientists discovered that her cells displayed certain characteristics never seen before; they actually could be multiplied many times over without dying. This meant that unlimited copies of her cells could be passed on. In the medical field, her cells were used to train new doctors and be part of experiments for groundbreaking treatments that eventually led to huge breakthroughs in cancer research. Even today, over 50 years later, her cells are still living, multiplying and being used to affect the world of medicine.

I believe that our lives can all be lived in a way that, no matter if we live for 19 years or for 109 years, the ripple effect of God's work can and will go on forever. God's power is known to work this way. When we work in accordance with His will for our lives, we are more than just meaningless, powerless people restricted by situations and circumstances. In God's power, we can say and do things that can ultimately reach and affect millions. God is the ultimate amplifier. How we choose to align with God's purpose for us determines whether our lives here get amplified for His glory or muted.

The danger is that we can choose to be scared of the stuff around us that we have no answer for and allow fear to make us stagnant. We can choose to never truly try to master or drive the vehicle we were blessed with. I know the phrase "Jesus, take the wheel" is well known in our culture but I prefer to say "Jesus *guide* the wheel." I'm the one who has to hop in the seat and start this bad boy up and go. God loves me enough to guide me along the trip, it's my job to trust Him... We need to actively drive our lives, but we also have to let God be the navigator.

In the Bible, when Jesus appeared on the water and told Peter to walk towards Him, he was asking Peter to *do the work* to come towards Him. Because walking towards Jesus meant walking on the water, Jesus was also asking that Peter trust Him to empower him for this task. Those steps are a microcosm of our daily challenge. Two requests you need to fulfill are:

1. Step out and drive.
2. Trust Him.

Peter began walking on the water towards Jesus. Then he started to stumble and drown when he took his eyes off of Jesus and focused on the treacherous waters around him.

I believe God is waiting for you to do the things He has empowered you to do, and a lot of you are sinking and drowning because you have shifted your focus off of Him. You have been looking around at the treacherous waters too long, letting fear cripple you. I pray that this book has provided some encouragement in your journey to take the next step. It's time to get up out of the backseat, hop in the driver's seat and start driving this thing called life.

Wrap-up

Use the pages to set a goal and check in over time.

My Make and Model!
When it comes to being one of God's useful tools, I am a(n):

_____

_____

Because:_____

_____

_____

_____

_____

_____

Plan the trip!
I want to start "driving my life" in this way:

_____

_____

_____

_____

_____

_____

_____

_____

_____

_____

_____

_____

_____

_____

_____

_____

_____

_____

Passengers!

The following people are affected by the way I choose to drive:

_____

_____

_____

_____

_____

_____

_____

Check-in!

30 days reading this, I'm:

_____

_____

_____

_____

_____

_____

_____

_____

_____

_____

_____

_____

_____

_____

Milestones/Praise Reports!
I thank God for the growth I've had in:

_____

_____

_____

_____

_____

_____

_____

_____

_____

_____

_____

_____

About the Author

Jay Floyd is a husband, father, motivational speaker and life coach. His testimony is one of gut-wrenching pain and heart-warming redemption. After experiencing the loss of nearly every family member he grew up with, he was able to recognize God's hand in his life and seek His healing touch. Known for his passionate stage presence and booming voice, he speaks and coaches from a message of "God-centered assertive engagement" as a way to better manifest God's will for our lives. He volunteers at New Community Bible Fellowship in University Heights, OH. He lives outside of Cleveland, OH with his wife Dennia and three children: Juliet, Honor and Jason Jr.

Printed in Great Britain
by Amazon